I0605374

HAUNTED PLACES

# HAUNTED ASYLUMS & HOSPITALS

by Richard Sebra

BrightPoint Press

San Diego, CA

an imprint of ReferencePoint Press, Inc.
Printed in the United States

For more information, contact:
BrightPoint Press
PO Box 27779
San Diego, CA 92198
www.BrightPointPress.com



LIBRARY OF CONGRESS CATALOGING-IN-PUBLICATION DATA

Name: Sebra, Richard, author.
Title: Haunted asylums & hospitals / by Richard Sebra.
Description: San Diego, CA: ReferencePoint Press, 2026 | Series: Haunted places | Audience: Grade 7 to 9 | Includes bibliographical references and index.
Identifiers: ISBN: 9781678211783 (hardcover) | ISBN: 9781678211790 (eBook)
The complete Library of Congress record is available at www.loc.gov.

# CONTENTS

# AT A GLANCE

- Many asylums and hospitals around the world are thought to be haunted. These places may have long, dark histories.

- People believe there are many reasons why ghosts haunt asylums and hospitals. Patients may have died unexpectedly, they may have suffered when they were alive, or they might not realize they are dead.

- Evidence of a haunting could include changes in temperature, unexplained voices or footsteps, objects moving by themselves, and shadowy figures.

- People have reported unexplained activity in asylums and hospitals across the United States. Waverly Hills Sanatorium is one of the most famous haunted locations.

- Other supposedly haunted hospitals include Trans-Allegheny Lunatic Asylum, Rolling Hills Asylum, and Essex Mountain Sanatorium.

- Ghost hunters visit places believed to be haunted. They use special tools and equipment to search for evidence of spirits.

- Ghost tours have become popular attractions. People can explore spooky buildings, stay overnight, or do their own investigation.

# GHOSTS OF THE PAST

The wind howled through broken windows. Rain pounded on the worn ceiling. It leaked through rusted holes. The only light in Waverly Hills **Sanatorium** came from a flashlight. A man and woman were investigating the hospital in Louisville, Kentucky. They had heard many creepy stories about it. They decided to look for evidence that it was haunted.

**Many patients suffered and died while at Waverly Hills Sanatorium. The treatments they received were often cruel and dangerous.**

**The tunnel under Waverly Hills was used to move the bodies of dead patients out of the building.**

The two turned a corner. The woman felt uneasy. The temperature in the room seemed to change. She felt as though she walked through a patch of cold air. Suddenly, a door slammed across the hall. They were the only people there. The wind did not seem strong enough to shut the heavy door. The woman moved her flashlight. What looked to be a moving shadow caught her attention.

The two continued walking down a long hallway. But the woman quickly stopped. She saw the **silhouette** of a person standing at the end of the hall. The figure appeared to be wearing a long doctor's coat. Before she could call out, the figure disappeared. The woman wondered whether it was a person or a ghost.

**Reports of humanlike figures, cold spots, and the unexplained sounds of footsteps are common at supposedly haunted places.**

# ASYLUM AND HOSPITAL HAUNTINGS

**Abandoned** buildings often seem mysterious and spooky. Places such as old hospitals and asylums can be especially creepy. They may have been around for hundreds of years. Their walls hold countless memories. And many of those memories are painful.

Patients die in hospitals every day. Some people believe that a person's spirit remains in the place where they died. Stories of haunted hospitals and asylums come from around the world. Ghost hunters investigate these stories. They look for evidence of ghosts. They try to prove whether asylums and hospitals are haunted.

Many old and abandoned hospitals around the world are believed to be haunted. These places may have dark histories.

# CHAPTER ONE

# PLACES OF SUFFERING

For hundreds of years, people have claimed that places are haunted. There are supposedly haunted mansions, hotels, and even ships. But hospitals are one of the most common places where people report ghosts. Asylums are also thought to be haunted. These are hospitals that treat people with **mental illnesses**.

Hospitals and asylums are thought to be haunted for several reasons. Some people

**While many hospitals that are thought to be haunted are abandoned, ghostly experiences are also reported at hospitals that are still open.**

feel uncomfortable inside them. People usually only go to these places if they have to. They may go if they are sick. Or they may visit a loved one. Hospitals are often associated with pain and suffering.

## WHY GHOSTS HAUNT

People have many beliefs as to why ghosts would haunt a place. Strong emotions are

**Many cultures and religions believe a person's spirit leaves their body when they die.**

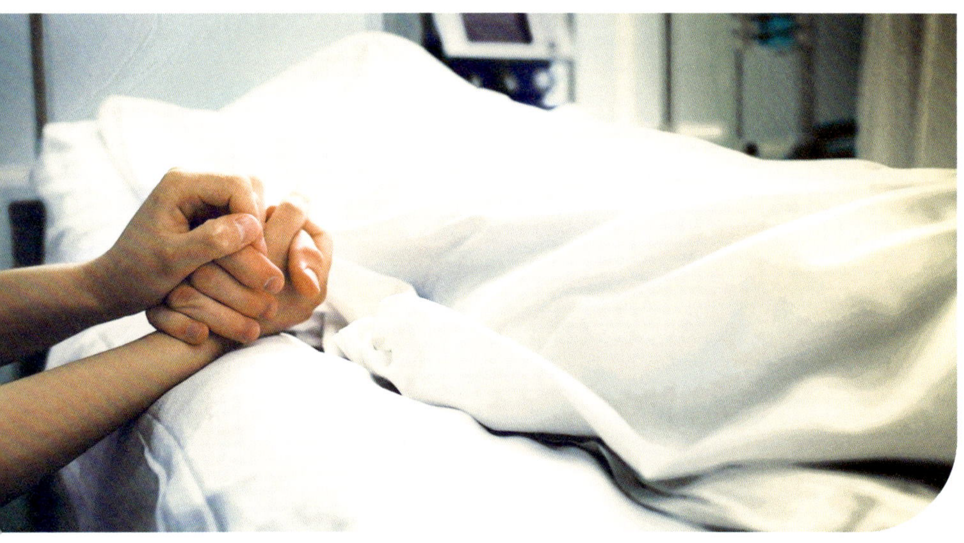

one reason. A person's spirit might remain if they experienced strong emotions as they died. The ghost may want something. This could be revenge for what happened during its life. It might be trying to warn others of danger. Or the ghost may not realize it died.

A violent death could also cause a spirit to haunt a place. Death and suffering are common at hospitals. Patients might suffer from illnesses or bad injuries. Suffering also occurs in asylums. People with mental illnesses sometimes stay at an asylum for many years.

Any hospital or asylum could be haunted. Nurses and patients often report mysterious activity. Old hospitals are especially thought to be haunted. This could be because of the setting. Abandoned hospitals are dark, quiet, and falling apart. There could be old equipment still inside. They feel creepy. People may imagine ghosts in the shadows.

Old hospitals and asylums are also thought to be haunted because of their past. They were often where people went to die. Some people would go to a hospital due to a deadly illness. Others went because they were injured in a war. Some old medical treatments

## Haunted Woods

**Not all haunted hospitals are in a building. During the American Civil War (1861–1865), injured soldiers were treated outdoors. These are known as field hospitals. The Battle of Gettysburg was fought in Gettysburg, Pennsylvania. Soldiers were treated in the nearby woods. Today, these woods are said to be haunted.**

made patients sicker. They also caused some patients to die. So old hospitals were the homes for many deaths.

Mental health treatment at old asylums was also limited. The understanding of mental illness was poor. Treatment often did more harm than good. Asylum patients suffered a lot in the early days of medicine. This could have affected them as they died. Their spirits may not have been able to move on after death.

## SIGNS OF A HAUNTING

Many people report having **paranormal** experiences. They believe these prove that a place is haunted. The temperature in a room may feel colder. Some people may report unexplained smells and sounds.

Lights might flicker on and off. Doors may open and close by themselves.

Reports of unexplained footsteps are also common. Some people have even claimed to see ghosts. The ghost may look like a shadowy figure. It could look like an orb. These experiences can be shocking. People share them with others. These stories fascinate people. They make people wonder whether they are true.

Ghost hunters will investigate these reports. They look for other kinds of evidence to prove a place is haunted. Ghost hunting attempts to use more scientific methods to find this evidence. Many theories try to explain the ways ghosts show themselves. However, there is no scientific evidence that ghosts exist.

Several famous haunted hospitals and asylums are found in the United States. Many of these places are abandoned. But some haunted hospitals are still open. Other countries also have supposedly haunted places. No matter the location, the paranormal fascinates people.

**Morgues are rooms in hospitals where dead bodies are temporarily stored. Some people think morgues are hot spots for ghostly activity.**

# CHILLING ENCOUNTERS

Tales of hauntings have been passed down for generations. Some early tales appeared in books. People also talked to each other about unexplained events. Today, people often share their paranormal experiences online. These stories make people want to learn more about these places.

The Waverly Hills Sanatorium opened in 1910. It was built to treat patients

**Traverse City State Hospital is considered one of the most haunted places in Michigan.**

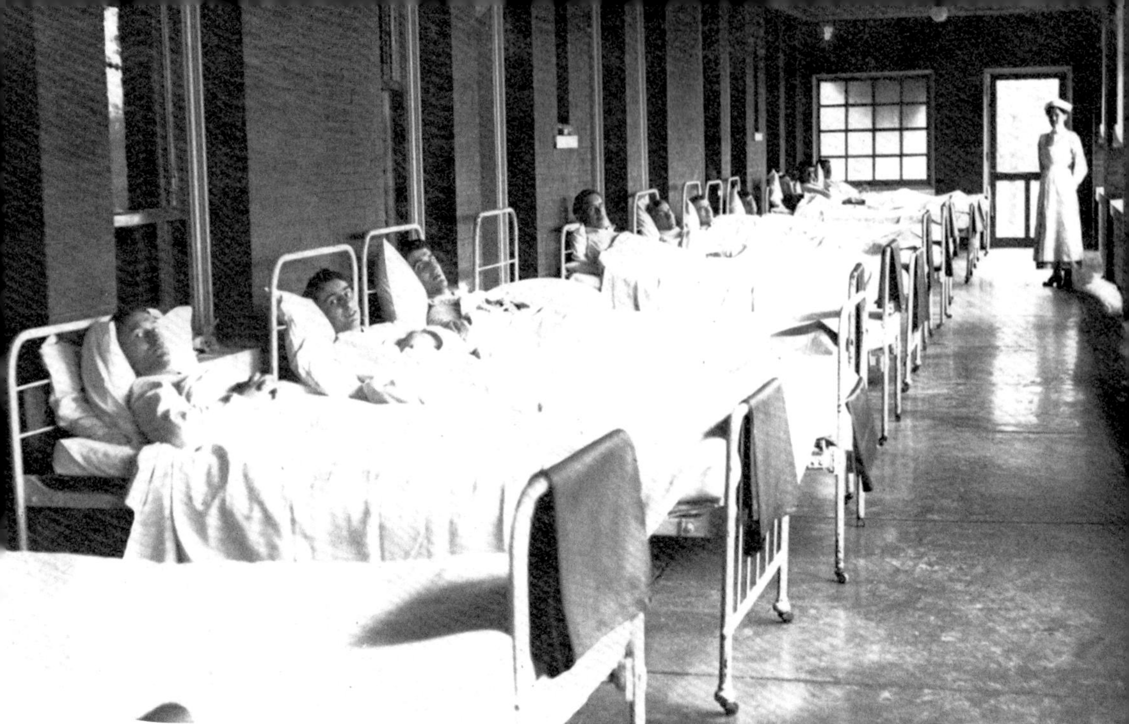

**Sanatoriums were often overcrowded during the 1900s. This meant patients were sometimes put in beds in the hallways.**

with tuberculosis. This is a lung disease. In the early 1900s, tuberculosis could not be cured. The hospital saw lots of death. Some rumors claim that more than 60,000 people died there.

Waverly Hills closed in 1961. Since then, many people have claimed it is haunted. Some people have reported hearing unexplained screams. There are also stories of shadowy figures. Some people have reported seeing the ghost of a doctor. He is seen on the fourth floor.

In 2001, Charlie Mattingly and his wife bought the building. They planned to fix it up and open it to the public. Mattingly noticed strange activity in Waverly Hills right away. "First time I walked in the building, I felt something very, very odd," he said.[1]

On one of his first visits, Mattingly took video of the building. When he reviewed it later, he saw floating orbs in the video. Another time, Mattingly was walking down the hallways. He suddenly heard voices. He went to the door of the room where he heard them. Mattingly jumped into the room and shouted. He used his flashlight to look around. But nobody was in the room.

The building eventually started being fixed up. While there, workers heard odd noises. Doors slammed by themselves. A shadowy man was seen in the hallways. Visitors reported similar things once the building was opened. Today, Waverly Hills is considered one of the most haunted hospitals in the United States.

## A CHILL UP THE SPINE

Essex Mountain Sanatorium is located in Cedar Grove, New Jersey. It is also known as the Hilltop. This is because it sits on a hill. The hospital opened in the late 1800s. It treated people with mental illnesses. Then in the early 1900s, it started treating tuberculosis patients. The building was eventually abandoned.

Some people believed a few patients stayed behind after the hospital closed. The patients were said to live there. That added to the stories of the hospital being haunted.

There are many reports of paranormal activity at Essex Mountain. Some people have claimed to see the ghosts of children.

**Medical equipment and tools were sometimes left behind when an asylum or hospital was abandoned.**

**Paranormal experts say that the spirits of children can be playful and very active.**

They are seen walking around the third floor. Unexplained footsteps and sounds have been reported. People also say they see wheelchairs and other things move on their own.

Today, the hospital is still abandoned. But that has not stopped visitors from exploring it. Mark Moran is one such explorer. For years, Moran had heard rumors that Essex Mountain was haunted. So he decided to visit. The place seemed creepy to him. It was falling apart. There was also old medical equipment throughout.

During his visit, Moran came to the end of a long hallway. He looked down and noticed his footprints in the dust. He then looked to where he had not walked yet. That was when he saw a single footprint in the dust. "All of a sudden I began to feel

## Topeka State Hospital

**Topeka State Hospital is located in Topeka, Kansas. It was once known as Topeka Insane Asylum. The hospital was open from 1872 until 1997. It took in people considered mentally ill. Many patients suffered and died there. Today, the hospital is believed to be haunted. People say the ghosts of those who died there haunt the building and the cemetery outside it.**

very vulnerable," said Moran. "I froze for a moment. . . . A shiver ran the length of my spine as I stood there in the diminishing light."[2] Moran decided to leave after that.

Other visitors had similar ghostly experiences. A local band was once taking pictures on the property. When they later looked at the photos, a strange mist appeared in one of them. They claimed to see the face of a screaming woman in the mist.

## GROWING UP WITH GHOSTS

The Danvers State Hospital opened in 1878. It is in Danvers, Massachusetts. The building is considered one of the most haunted asylums in the world. Danvers State Hospital stopped treating patients

**Danvers State Hospital was previously named Danvers Insane Hospital.**

in 1992. But people remain fascinated by its history.

Many bad things occurred at the hospital. People suffered through painful, experimental treatments. These included brain surgeries and shock therapy. The hospital was also overcrowded. Some people were forced to stay in the building's basement. In 1939, nearly 300 patients died. Many of them were buried in the cemeteries on the hospital's grounds. During the 1980s, some patients started mysteriously disappearing. More than 100 patients were once said to have disappeared within a 3-month period.

Jeralyn Levasseur grew up in a house on the grounds of Danvers. Her father worked at the hospital. Levasseur experienced unexplained events while living there. She said lights would flicker on and off. She claimed to see the figure of a woman in the attic. The covers on her bed were once ripped off as she slept.

Levasseur believes the ghosts of the people who suffered still haunt the hospital. She said, "If you think back to the beginnings of medical science and the things done to people . . . you have to wonder, did people think they were being tortured?"[3]

Today, the hospital is abandoned. But people still visit in the hopes of experiencing something paranormal. Visitors often report feeling a strange energy. Some believe it is due to the many people who suffered there.

**During the 1800s and 1900s, many patients at mental asylums were restrained as a form of treatment or so they would not escape.**

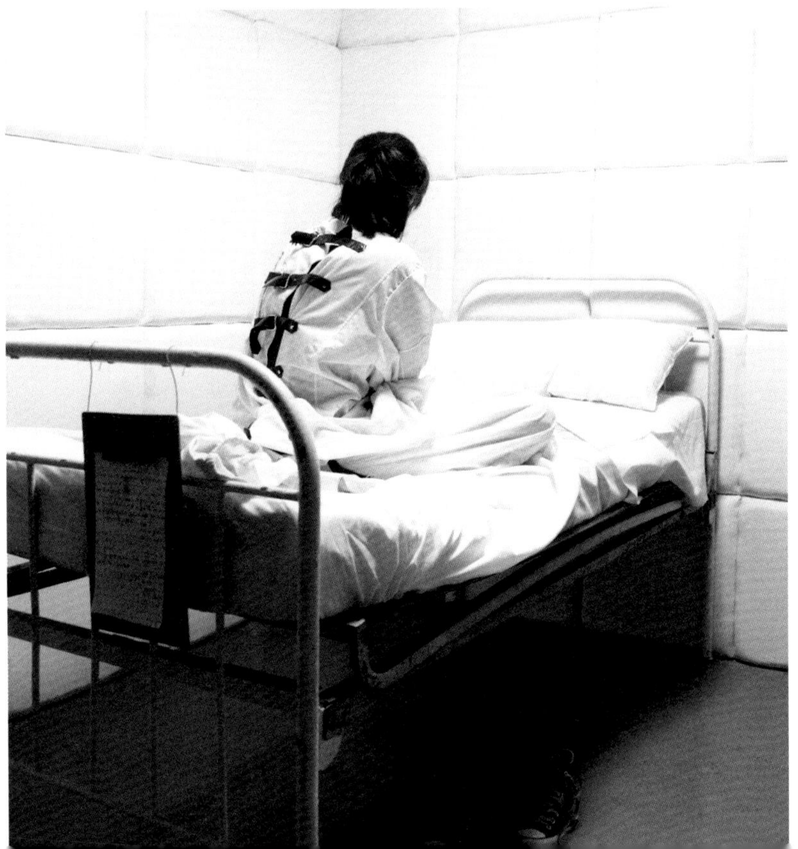

# HUNTING SPIRITS

Haunted asylums and hospitals are frightening to many people. But some want to find proof that these places are haunted. Ghost hunters are also known as paranormal investigators. They visit the world's most haunted places. They look for evidence of the paranormal. Some ghost hunters share their experiences on TV shows. Others may share them online.

**Ghost hunters travel across the United States to investigate supposedly haunted locations.**

Paranormal investigators believe spirits use and release energy. This energy shows when spirits interact with **electromagnetic** fields (EMFs). Electrical charges generate EMFs. A ghost's energy is said to interfere with these fields. This can be measured on ghost hunting devices. Investigators use detectors and meters that measure the strength of an EMF. "A sudden, unexplained spike in EMF readings is often considered evidence of a potential paranormal presence by ghost hunters," says electrical engineer Marina Antoniou.[4]

A spirit box is another piece of ghost hunting equipment. This device scans radio signals. Some people believe that ghosts can use these signals to communicate. Spirits may make noises that people cannot hear in real time. Ghost hunters use special recorders to try to capture these sounds.

## GHOSTLY NURSE

Ghost hunter Ronnie Dee owns Old South Pittsburg Hospital Paranormal Research Center (OSPHPRC). It is located near Chattanooga, Tennessee. The building opened during the late 1950s. It used to

### Ghost Hunters on Screen

Ghost hunting TV shows have become very popular. The show *Ghost Hunters* began airing in 2004. It allowed people to see what a paranormal investigation was like. Since then, many other ghost hunting shows have come out. These include *Ghost Adventures* and *Paranormal Lockdown*. There are also ghost hunting videos on YouTube.

**A residual haunting is said to occur when the energy from an emotional event leaves a ghostly impression on the living world.**

be a community hospital. The hospital shut down in 1998. Today, the building is a base for ghost hunting.

Steve Nelson is a ghost hunter. He has done several investigations at OSPHPRC. One time, Nelson and his sister were walking through the building. It was daytime. Nelson's sister recorded a video. They later reviewed it. In it, they saw the figure of a nurse. "You can tell because of the hat, the nurse hat," said Nelson. "She had the dress on and everything, and whenever she moved, it was clear."[5]

Today, OSPHPRC is believed to be one of the most haunted places in Tennessee. Some visitors say they have heard babies crying there. Others have heard unexplained voices. Some have even claimed to be touched by a spirit. There are also reports of people seeing the ghosts of former patients and doctors.

## A FLICKERING LIGHT

The Trans-Allegheny Lunatic Asylum is located in Weston, West Virginia. It opened in the mid-1800s. The asylum was designed to house 250 patients. But it held as many as 2,400. It took in people suffering from a variety of disorders. The hospital shut down in 1994. Then in 2008, the building opened for ghost hunts and tours.

One paranormal investigator is Nora Fussner. In 2023, Fussner joined a group of ghost hunters on an investigation. She brought ghost hunting equipment. This included a digital voice recorder and an EMF reader. Someone also brought a radiating electromagnetic field pod, or REM pod. A REM pod is a device that measures temperature changes. It can detect fields of energy, too.

Some ghosts at Trans-Allegheny are called by a certain name. Frank and Larry used to be patients at the hospital. They were also said to be roommates. During the investigation, one ghost hunter

**Trans-Allegheny Lunatic Asylum is also known as Weston State Hospital.**

put a REM pod in Frank and Larry's room. He then placed a flashlight on the floor. The investigator asked the ghosts questions. The REM pod was constantly beeping. The flashlight also flickered.

The ghost hunter eventually asked Frank and Larry to leave. When he did, the beeping stopped. "As the flashlight flickers, untouched, we all feel a cool breeze move down the hallway," remembers Fussner. "As much as I want to be **skeptical** of the meters . . . I also want this, something that feels not possible."[6]

The investigators visited another room. It was believed to be haunted by a little girl. They put two balloons in the room. They asked the girl whether she wanted to play. Then one of the balloons moved. The investigators were standing in the hall when

**Ghost hunters review their audio and video recordings to check for evidence they might have missed during their investigation.**

this happened. They thought they might have made the balloon move. They walked around in the hall to see whether it would move again. But it did not.

## SEARCHING FOR EVIDENCE

Connecticut Paranormal Encounters and Research (CPEAR) investigates haunting reports. One investigation took place at Rolling Hills Asylum. The asylum is in East Bethany, New York. Rolling Hills has a long history. It first opened as housing for the poor during the 1800s. It later became a treatment center for people with mental illnesses.

The CPEAR team did an experiment in one of the rooms. A flashlight was placed on the floor. It was turned on. The team went into the hall. It wanted to see whether any ghostly activity would cause the light to flicker.

Nobody was in the room. But the light started fading as it might if someone were walking up to it. It even appeared as if the light was completely blocked. The flashlight had not flickered when it had been used before. The team could not explain the event.

The investigators also used digital audio recorders. One person tried to get the ghosts to go into the hallway. The team captured a voice that said, "You, go away!"

CPEAR co-founder Carrie Kerns also had a strange experience at Rolling Hills. She said, "Upon our arrival in the afternoon, I had felt a dizziness that had stayed with

**Rolling Hills Asylum is said to be home to many spirits, including a former resident named Roy and another named Hattie.**

me while we were there . . . and went away after we were in the car and left the area."[7]

Other ghost hunters have reported haunted experiences at Rolling Hills, too. They have recorded the sound of an organ playing. Some have also recorded voices. However, there is no proof that Rolling Hills or other hospitals are haunted. Even so, investigators continue searching for evidence.

# HAUNTED TOURS

Exploring haunted hospitals and asylums can be dangerous. Abandoned facilities are not usually open to the public. These buildings may be falling apart. People often have to get permission to visit these places. This is the case for both ghost hunters and those who just want to explore.

Many haunted hospitals and asylums welcome visitors. Ghost tours have become

**People can learn about the paranormal history of a location during a haunted tour.**

popular attractions. They allow people to explore these locations.

## A HISTORIC LANDMARK

One place people can visit is the Trans-Allegheny Lunatic Asylum. The asylum is a National Historic Landmark. This means it is considered important because of its history. Some people go there to learn more about that history. Others may go hoping to experience something paranormal.

Trans-Allegheny offers several ghost tours. These tours are guided. Some guides take visitors to the most haunted areas of the building. Visitors can go during the day or at night.

In 2018, Marisa Kashino visited the asylum. She decided to take part in an overnight ghost hunt. During the hunt, Kashino paired up with a woman named Julia. They went into a room that was said to be haunted by a ghost named Jim James. Julia put a flashlight on the ground. The two asked Jim to turn it on.

**Ghost hunt tours at Trans-Allegheny Lunatic Asylum allow visitors to explore all 242,000 square feet (22,500 sq m) of the building.**

Suddenly, the light turned on. The women then offered a gift to Jim if he turned the light off. Suddenly, the flashlight turned off by itself.

Kashino and Julia then explored other rooms. They tried to get the flashlight to turn on and off by itself again. But it did not happen. Kashino could not explain

## Hospitals in Movies

**Abandoned hospitals are sometimes used as settings for movies or TV shows. Their spooky vibes can be the perfect place for a scary story. The Linda Vista Hospital in Los Angeles, California, was used to film several movies and TV shows. During filming, some people reported seeing moving shadows and hearing strange noises. This led them to believe the hospital was haunted.**

the experience. She said, "Maybe Jim James did turn on that flashlight. Or maybe there's some mechanical explanation. I just don't know—and what's more exciting than the unknowable?"[8]

## ON THE HUNT

Saint Ignatius Hospital is located in Colfax, Washington. Saint Ignatius was built in 1893. It closed as a hospital in 1968. The building is also called the Colfax Haunted Hospital. It is known for being haunted.

Some people have reported strange activity at the hospital. A shadowy black mass is said to attack visitors. They believe it could be an angry spirit. People have also claimed to hear unexplained voices and to see dark shadows. This strange activity drew the attention of ghost hunters. The hospital has appeared on several ghost hunting TV shows. This includes *Ghost Adventures*.

Saint Ignatius offers many kinds of tours. One tour gives people the opportunity to join a real ghost hunt. Guests are given ghost hunting equipment. They then can conduct their own investigation. A guide can help people during the investigation.

Valoree Gregory was a tour guide at the hospital. "After being in there just two times, I realized that it was really haunted," she said.[9] Gregory claimed to have many paranormal experiences at the hospital. This included recording strange voices. Visitors have also reported feeling uneasy in some of the hospital's rooms.

**The proceeds from the haunted tours at Saint Ignatius Hospital are used to help preserve the building.**

## EXPLORE THE UNKNOWN

Eloise Asylum is located in Westland, Michigan. The asylum was open from 1839 until 1982. It was once the largest **psychiatric** building in the United States. It had about 10,000 patients at one time. The spirits of those who died are said to still haunt the area. This includes the ghosts of two children. People also report seeing the ghost of a woman and a doctor there.

Today, the site offers many kinds of tours. These include tours guided by professional ghost hunters. The ghost hunting tours take

**Pennhurst Asylum in Spring City, Pennsylvania, has several haunted attractions in which actors dress up in creepy costumes.**

# FAMOUS HAUNTED ASYLUMS AND HOSPITALS IN THE UNITED STATES

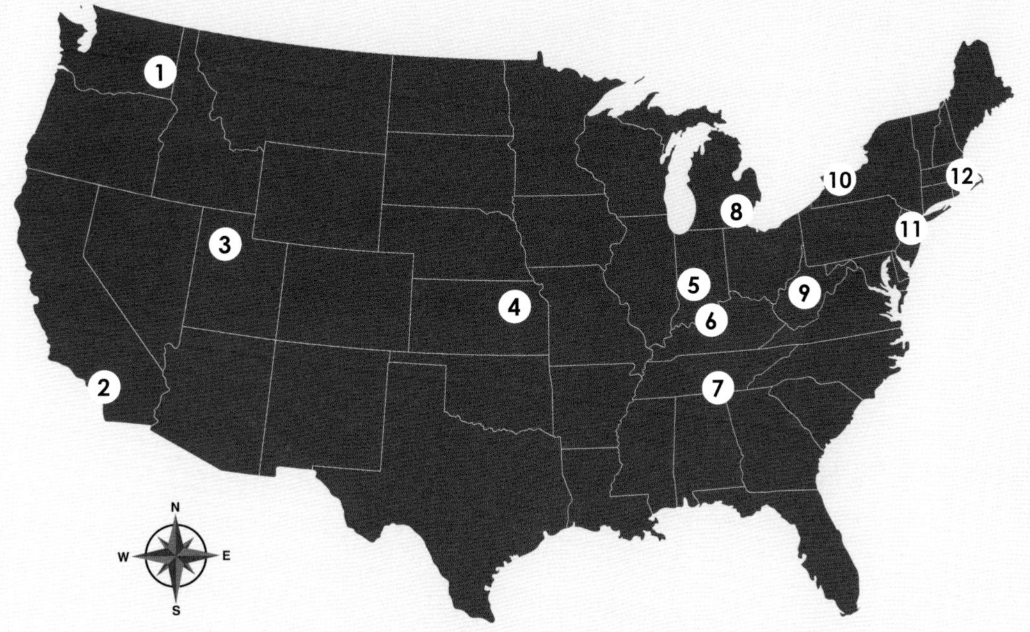


1. Saint Ignatius Hospital: Colfax, Washington
2. Linda Vista Hospital: Los Angeles, California
3. Asylum 49: Tooele, Utah
4. Topeka State Hospital: Topeka, Kansas
5. Indiana State Sanatorium: Rockville, Indiana
6. Waverly Hills Sanatorium: Louisville, Kentucky
7. Old South Pittsburg Hospital: Chattanooga, Tennessee
8. Eloise Asylum: Westland, Michigan
9. Trans-Allegheny Lunatic Asylum: Weston, West Virginia
10. Rolling Hills Asylum: East Bethany, New York
11. Essex Mountain Sanatorium: Cedar Grove, New Jersey
12. Danvers State Hospital: Danvers, Massachusetts

Many asylums and hospitals across the United States are believed to be haunted.

place overnight. Guests can bring their own equipment. Or they can be given equipment to use. Eloise Asylum also offers other activities, such as escape rooms.

The Indiana State Sanatorium is in Rockville, Indiana. It is one of the most popular haunted hospitals in the Midwest. The hospital treated everything from diseases to mental illness. It first ran from 1908 to 1968. It then became a nursing home from 1976 to 2011.

Many people have claimed to have paranormal experiences at Indiana State. Some say they heard strange sounds and voices. Reports of unexplained footsteps have been reported in a building called Adams Hall. And many have claimed to see shadowy figures wandering the hospital.

Indiana State offers several haunted tours. People can go on self-guided tours. They can explore all 120,000 square feet (11,150 sq m) of the building. Visitors also have the option of spending the night there. They can investigate during the overnight stay. Guests can use provided equipment to search for ghosts.

**Indiana State Sanatorium closed in 2011. Many ghost hunters have investigated the hospital since then.**

Tales of ghosts at hospitals and asylums continue to make people wonder whether these places are actually haunted.

Supposedly haunted asylums and hospitals have often seen a lot of pain and suffering. Many people have also died in these places. This dark history makes some people question whether these buildings are haunted. Strange things happen in these places. Ghost hunters explore them to find evidence of spirits. There is no proof that ghosts exist. But there is no doubt that people are fascinated by the paranormal.

# GLOSSARY

**abandoned**

no longer occupied

**electromagnetic**

having to do with a relationship between electricity and magnetic fields

**mental illnesses**

types of illnesses, such as depression, that affect people's thoughts, feelings, and behaviors

**paranormal**

something that is unexplained by science, such as ghosts or aliens

**psychiatric**

relating to the study and treatment of mental illness

**sanatorium**

also called a sanitarium, a type of hospital that offers long-term treatment for illnesses

**silhouette**

the dark outline of a body against something lighter

**skeptical**

doubtful or not easily convinced about something

# SOURCE NOTES

## CHAPTER TWO: CHILLING ENCOUNTERS

1. Quoted in Eric Jones, "Retro Find: 'Holy Grail of Haunted Houses' Was Once a Hospital Where Thousands Died," *KCRA*, September 28, 2023, 0:02. www.kcra.com.

2. Quoted in Mark and Mark, "Welcome to Hell: The Essex Mountain Sanatorium," *Weird N.J.*, August 26, 2013. https://weirdnj.com.

3. Quoted in Michael Puffer, "The Lore, and Lure, of Danvers State Hospital," *Festival of the Dead*, October 29, 2003. www.festivalofthedead.com.

## CHAPTER THREE: HUNTING SPIRITS

4. Quoted in "Ghost Hunting Equipment: What You Need to Know According to an Electricity Expert," *University of Warwick*, October 23, 2023. https://warwick.ac.uk.

5. Quoted in "Old South Pittsburg Hospital," *Phantom History*, n.d., 0:37. https://phantomhistory.com.

6. Nora Fussner, "A Visit to the Trans-Allegheny Asylum; Or, on Hauntings and History," *CrimeReads*, October 16, 2023. https://crimereads.com.

7. Quoted in "The Stories," *Rolling Hills Asylum*, n.d. www.rollinghillsasylum.com.

## CHAPTER FOUR: HAUNTED TOURS

8. Marisa M. Kashino, "I Spent the Night in a Haunted Asylum and I Still Can't Explain What I Saw," *Washingtonian*, October 25, 2018. www.washingtonian.com.

9. Quoted in Jared Brown, "TV Show Claims Proof of Ghosts at St. Ignatius Hospital in Colfax, but No Haunted Tours Scheduled," *Spokesman-Review*, June 18, 2019, 0:58. www.spokesman.com.

# FOR FURTHER RESEARCH

## BOOKS

Kenny Abdo, *Haunted Asylums*. Abdo Publishing, 2021.

Janie Havemeyer, *Haunted Houses & Mansions*. BrightPoint Press, 2026.

Carla Mooney, *Ghost Sightings*. BrightPoint Press, 2024.

## INTERNET SOURCES

"Ghost Hunting Equipment: What You Need to Know According to an Electricity Expert," *University of Warwick*, October 23, 2023. https://warwick.ac.uk.

"Haunted Massachusetts Hospitals: Taunton and Danvers," *Boston Ghosts*, January 26, 2021. https://bostonghosts.com.

"Top 10 Most Haunted Hospitals in the World," *US Ghost Adventures*, January 12, 2022. https://usghostadventures.com.

## WEBSITES

### Ghost City Tours

**https://ghostcitytours.com**

The Ghost City Tours site showcases ghost tours in several US cities. It also lists the most-haunted locations in each city and discusses the history of those places.

### Haunted Rooms America

**www.hauntedrooms.com**

Haunted Rooms America features haunted locations around the United States. The site includes a variety of places that are believed to be haunted, including asylums and hospitals, along with ghost tours that people can go on.

### Waverly Hills Sanatorium

**https://thewaverlyhillssanatorium.com**

This website explores the Waverly Hills Sanatorium. It features the history of the hospital along with the paranormal experiences that people have had there.

# INDEX

# IMAGE CREDITS

Cover: © Herbivora/Shutterstock Images
5: © sdecoret/Shutterstock Images
7: © KMiles4890/Shutterstock Images
8: © Aaron Vowels/Flickr
9: © Anki Hoglund/Shutterstock Images
11: © Declan Hillman/Shutterstock Images
13: © Andreas Gradin/Shutterstock Images
14: © Sfam_Photo/Shutterstock Images
19: © sutlafk/Shutterstock Images
21: © SamanthaB2022/Shutterstock Images
22: © chippix/Shutterstock Images
25: © MDWhitstable/Shutterstock Images
26: © Victoria OM/Shutterstock Images
29: © Kirk Williamson/Salem State Archives
31: © Alvaro German Vilela/Shutterstock Images
33: © Vladimir Mulder/Shutterstock Images
36: © lightkey/iStockphoto
39: © Malachi Jacobs/Shutterstock Images
40: © Kevin Kilhoffer/Journal Gazette/AP Images
43: © devnin/Shutterstock Images
45: © PhotopankPL/Shutterstock Images
47: © Carol M. Highsmith/Library of Congress
51: © Kirk Fisher/Shutterstock Images
52: © Don Valentine Photography/Shutterstock Images
53 (hospitals): © Muhamad_Khotibul_Umam/Shutterstock Images
53 (map): © Red Line Editorial
55: © Nagel Photography/Shutterstock Images
56: © Asukanda/Shutterstock Images

# ABOUT THE AUTHOR

Richard Sebra is a book author and journalist. He and his wife live in Vista, California, where they enjoy cooking, surfing, and hiking with their dogs.